*My Anthology
of
Poetry and Songs*

My Anthology
of
Poetry and Songs

By

Edward O. Eddy, Sr.

authorHOUSE®

AuthorHouse™ LLC
1663 Liberty Drive
Bloomington, IN 47403
www.authorhouse.com
Phone: 1-800-839-8640

Published by AuthorHouse 08/25/2014

ISBN: 978-1-4969-3460-4 (sc)
ISBN: 978-1-4969-3499-4 (hc)
ISBN: 978-1-4969-3500-7 (e)

Library of Congress Control Number: 2014914716

Author's Note

*I have been inspired by **God**, my family, friends, inspired me and the women I have put into verse feelings ad awareness brought about through our interactions. It is my hope that these verses will inspire the readers to examine themselves and their lives to expand their spirituality and enter new frontiers in their personal relationships.*

Edward Eddy

Dedication and Acknowledgments

*Firstly, this is dedicated to the **LORD GOD** for his inspiration and unfailing love.*

*Also to my family and friends who supported me throughout my endeavor to create this collection. Without their love, help and inspiration this would not have been possible. Special thanks **Ms. Betty L. Mahoney** for helping with obtaining the grant. Thanks **Mr. Alfred Haynes** for assisting with the art work for the book cover. Also final thanks to **Tyra U De Castro** and **Tinika Christopher** for their administrative work.*

Thank you, all of you,

Sincerely,

Edward o. Eddy, Sr.

Table of Contents

Tainted

People will try to paint a picture that's not true,
But **God** will be able to see you through
Whatever you've done in darkness
must come to light
If we only trust **God** and keep
His promise in our sight.

They say never judge a book by its cover,
To open it is to realize what glory we can discover
So why should I judge my sister or brother
When I don't know what's under the cover.

You see the picture they just painted.
It started off bad because it was tainted.
Now I know what I'll do, I will repaint
The picture of the real you.

Haters

Why do some people to tend to hate?
They know their own lives are not straight.
They're only showing the love they lack
When they talk about you, behind your back

Smiling in your face like everything O.K
Lie instead of saying what they want to say.
Coming at you with all these lame games,
They only hope to bring you pain and shame.

There is many people that act that way
Scheming and tricking the livelong day
Here's one thing I advise you to do
Look in the mirror and see if that's you!

Copyright@ 09/28/2006 Edward Eddy

Changing Faces

Faces I perceive change very day,
Could it be a reality of what they say?
I look around and it's plain to see,
That these faces don't deceive me...

Some smile and some frown
Giving you illusions that are s profound
Give me guidance, my **Creator**, in what to do
So I could see the true light of You...

In Your Word we were made in Your likeness
To reflect on Your holy brightness.
Faces I see change every day
Careful they do not lead you stray...

By: Edward Eddy, 5/19/05

Deceit

We see something glitter; we think its gold,
The real truth is, another lie has been told.
To us the grass is greener on the other side,
We are sure that it will change how we feel inside.

Not knowing Satan has fed us another lie,
We run off chasing that, "Pie in the Sky".
Looking for treasure in all the wrong places,
Destroying ourselves running too many races.

The glitter fills us up, makes our minds whirl,
We've lost sight of what really matters in the world.
For a little pleasure, we've sold our soul,
Losing it for something we thought was gold!

By Edward Eddy

I Could Not See

I don't know why I could not see
What that lady was doing to me.

I don't know why I could not see
She was destroying me mentally and physically.

I don't know why I could not see
That lady was bringing me to my knees.

I don't know why I could not see
That she came from an unstable family.

I don't know why I could not see
The lady lusted for others as well as me.

I don't know why I could not see
She flirted with others and was unfaithful to me.

I don't know why I could not see
That she was never meant for a man like me.

By: Edward Eddy 09/26/96

Mesmerize

I'm mesmerized by the spell of your beauty,
Gazing longingly into your lovely eyes.
Tantalized by the shape of your body,
I madly desire you, that's no surprise.

Sweet sensual beauty so lovely to view,
Your precious smile, soft as the dew.
Worth much more than silver and gold,
Like an angel, you're lovely to behold.

The outward things any sculptor can do,
They are not what makes you whole.
The true masterpiece that dwells in you,
Is the beauty of your heavenly soul.

By Edward Eddy © 11/29/2006

The Eyes of A Man

If the eyes of a man
Can enjoy its view
It would be his own pleasure
Of loving you.

And my eyes miss nothing
Even inside you I can see,
That there's a beautiful woman
That belongs to me.

To a flower you're even more beautiful
More precious than a pot of gold.
And I see your love is given
Never to be bought nor sold.

Beauty is in the eye of the beholder
At least that's what people say
But the only thing I see for myself
I love you each and every day.

By: Edward Eddy 1/20/1997

What I Like About You

I like the way you walk
I like the way you talk

I like the way you sway
I like the things you say

I like to get next to you
I like the things you do

I like the way you smile
I like your class and style

I like the way you move so sweet
I also like your sexy feet

But what I like most is your smell
Because it puts me in a spell

Written by Edward © Eddy 12/02/06

"No Matter The Cost"

My yoke is easy, my burden is light
Because Jesus paid the ultimate price
If you see it, you can achieve it.
Put your heart in it and receive it.

No matter the cost, Jesus is boss
Hold you head up high, be strong,
It won't be long, no matter the cost
I was lost but now I am found.

Realizing my life is heaven bound
Jesus has never let us down
And I will be happy to wear the crown
No matter the cost

CHRISTMAS

Christmas is a time for sharing and caring,
A time for joy and peace in our hands
With the joyous smiles we are wearing
We'll make loving caring new starts.

As we travel on our merry way,
Let love and joy never cease.
Take time out or someone and pray
That everyone will be at peace.

Always remember deep in your heart
As we unfold the holiday season
Near at heart, or far apart
Out Savior Jesus is the reason.

When loved ones seem so far away
The lights and mistletoe
We're celebrating this Christmas day
With the love and joy of Him.

By Edward Eddy ©11/29/06

Mind Your Own Business

What I Do is none of your concern
Why don't you mind your business?
That's a lesson you will never learn,
You're too full of "Me - ness."

Mind your own business.

Time for you to leave gossip alone
Take care of your own affairs,
Get you a life to call your own,
Look inside for love you can share.

Mind your own business.

Quit meddling around in other's lives
You'll have trouble and trouble quick,
Breaking up homes, telling hateful lies
You'll get no trust, you peep the lick.

Mind your own business.

Women are nice if their your own
Sweet, tender and fun to kiss,
By other men's you leave alone,
They're not for you, you understand this?

Written by Edward Eddy © 05/10/05

Look Inside

Our life is just a big charade
Even though we smile and parade.
Fill with envy and pride
A dark depression deep inside

Though at times we smile
The smile is really just a mask
Worn to hide what is true and real
The inner child we all conceal

Help me to find the ways of truth
Let me look deep inside you
You have a peace I don't understand
Won't you please just take my hand?

Lead me in the way that I should go
Without guidance I just don't know
Where is darkness, where is light
How do I know what is just and right?

You found your peace in Jesus arms
Not in the world within its harms
Now show me what I have to do
To love with Jesus just like you

By Edward Eddy

I Want You To Love Me

I want you to love me like I love you
My days were saddened without you
I'm so glad that I found you.

You bring sunshine in m y life
That's why I want you to be my wife.
We'll be together 'til the end of time
Baby, to me you are so divine.

And the loving you've given to me
Captures my heart, sets me free.
You keep my world spinning around
I can't tell my ups from downs.

By Edward Eddy

Get Well Soon

When bodies ache
And you're feeling blue
I send my prayers
To comfort you.

I pray your health
Will soon be better
And comfort you'll find
Within my letter.

So le back and rest
Be comforted too
By all the things
Jesus does for you.

Special Day

On this very special day
There are a few words I would like to convey...

I must say congratulations!
To you and your new relation
I wish you the very best in life
I know he will be honored to have you as his wife.

I wish you all the happiness
Because is about togetherness
I know you will be blessed
Because your husband is looking for the best.

The love and compassion that
you have in your heart
It shows me that **God** is always a part
The way you care for other people's needs
It shows me that **God** will always be pleased.

Wishing you both a prosperous life
Living each day as husband and wife
There's no limit to what you can do together
Because of your faith, there is no measure.

By Edward Eddy © 01/05/07

My Every Desire

You are so fine.
I would like to make you mine
Your body is like poetry in motion
Sending out signals that arouse my emotions.

How lovely are you lips
Fine thighs and shapely hips
That fill me with desire
And set my blood on fire

Round and luscious and apple sweet
Your breasts are such a wondrous treat
Like honey flowing from the hive
Until there's nothing left to lose

Let's sail away on love's desire
And set each other's hearts afire
Our love is a consuming flame
Quenched by desire all the same

By Edward Eddy © 02/16/07

Feast of Desire

Biting into an apple, so good to eat,
The sweet juices run down my chin.
I think of you, love, soft and sweet,
All the pleasures that we shared back then

Like ripened red plums, kissed by the sun,
Your full lips were so luscious and moist.
Kisses, like grapes, I can't take just one,
I'm intoxicated by the grace of your voice.

The gently swelling globes of your lovely breasts,
Like two perfect melons of rare earthly delight.
Smooth slope of hip, the junction of thighs
Where I feasted on sweet nectar at night

The wine of love, from the rarest vines
Gets better with the passage of years.
Your memory lives in this vineyard of mine
That is watered only with my reverent tears.

By Edward Eddy © 02/06/07

Happy Valentine Mother

I want to say Happy Valentines
To a lady who is genuine
More than a mother, you're a friend
My steady anchor till the end
Because you and I can relate
Being your son is really great
You're more precious than gems to me
My Valentine you'll always be
You're so fine in every way
Wishing you a Happy Valentine's Day.

By Edward Eddy © 02/02/07

Happy Valentine Sister

I want to say Happy Valentines
To a sister who is genuine
You are more precious than gems
You're more than a sister, friend,
God made you the perfect blend
Because you and I can relate
Being your brother is really great
I think you are very fine
So have a Happy Valentines

By Edward Eddy © 02/02/07

Happy Valentine Lady

I want to say Happy Valentines
To a lady who is genuine
More than an acquaintance, you're a friend
Love and warmth in perfect blend
Being with you I can relate
That is why I choose you for my mate
I think you are very fine
So won't you be my Valentine?

By Edward Eddy © 02/02/07

Woman Stay

You're the woman who kindles my fire;
You're the one that I truly desire;
You're most definitely one of a kind;
So lovely, so precious; rare and refined.

You're striking beauty, so attractive it's alarming;
Makes you see as especially charming.
Can I capture a woman like you?
What's this poor man supposed to do?

Everything you are and everything you do
Creates perfection; keeps me twisted in you.
I'm not complaining; just asking you see;
Hoping and praying you'll stay with me

By Edward Eddy © 02/02/07

Mother's Care

To a mother who cares,
With so much to share.
When tines seem though,
And everything gets rough,
I know you're always there...

Mom, you soothe my fears,
And brush away my tears.
When the world is cold,
And darkness fills my soul,
Your heart is always near...

Your touch like an angel's wings,
Lifts me up, and my heart sings
Thinking of the things, you do,
I thank **God** for a mother like you,
And to you my heart clings...

My face I lift, my voice I raise,
And sing for you, this song of praise
This song I sing with heartfelt pleasure,
My love for you knows no measure,
God *gave me you, mom to bless my days.*

By Edward Eddy, 9/7/06

Outlook

Sometimes we laugh and sometimes we cry
And there comes a time we have to die
We have been in pain, and that's no lie
Can someone please tell me why?

For many years we've been deprived f our rights
We were unable to read and write
Because their hearts were filled
with segregation and strife
They ignore that **God** is the provider of your life

Dr. King started the flight; it's not accomplished
Let's pick up his spirit so his work
will not go unfinished
We must stand up and rise from mental slavery
And continue on with the reform of the King's legacy

This is not what democracy stands for
Corruption, degradation, exploitation
are this nation's core
It's better to be in Communism
Than living in a society of hidden racism.

The color of your skin is your passport
In U.S. equality, for the Black, there is no port
The tactic is to provide division
Which will leave us in total confusion

Without unity we have no solution
Which enables us to have a revolution
We need education to learn our rights
Because without knowledge we cannot fight

Put down pornography, music and lies on television
Learn about rights, and you will have a vision
So we can be no longer a puppet on a string
Be free to have a dream, and do your thing

Edward Eddy © 10/04/07

Dedication to Ms. Mathis

Ms. Mathis is a teacher who really cares
Her knowledge and wisdom she readily shares.
Ms. Mathis, you give us a great sense of hope
You help us to learn many good ways to cope.

You're more than just a teacher; you're a friend,
With wisdom, you guide us to truly comprehend.
You always make the time to lend us a hand,
At your worst, you don't offend,
you help us understand.

Ms Mathis is a teacher who strives not to neglect
She always shows her students the utmost respect
As a teacher, she is someone we can appreciate
Her family, friends and students
all know she is great!

The work you do with us is simply incredible
You're really one person who is totally unforgettable
Your departure will leave us in sad regret,
Yet the memories of you will never forget.

As you go on your way, you have the love of us all
Remember you're the one who taught us to stand tall
You carry part of your hearts and a lot of love
May you be eternally blessed by out Creator above.

By Edward Eddy 01/22/07

My Number One

Chorus 2x   You're my number one
             And you're the only one

Vs. 1   The more I love you
             It's like sweet, sweet wine
             And girl you know
             It gets better in time

Chorus 2x   You're my number one
             And you're the only one

Vs. 2   Your love is truly rare
             It's not about your skin tone and hair

bridge   I'm so glad that you are there
             Because I know you truly care.

Now put your hands on your hips
And me see you dip
Now wind up
Now work up harder

I love you when you dance
You put me in a trance
Can't wait to get the chance
To show you some romance

Written by Edward Eddy © 11/12/06

Got To Be Careful

Chorus 2x Got to be careful today
Got to find a better way...

Vs 1   Got to be careful of the
things people say
Lots of bad people getting in your way
Make you so angry with
the games they play
You want to shoot them,
blow them away.

Chorus 2x Got to be careful today
Got to find a better way...

Bridge	*Too much stealing and too much killing*
	Black on black crimes
	seem so appealing
	But you know brother,
	*that's not **God**'s way*
	Love them instead just kneel and pray
Chorus 2x	*Got to be careful today*
	Got to find a better way...
Vs 3	*Raise up your children in the right way*
	Then they will never, go
	running astray
	Trusting in Jehovah each
	step of the way
	Don't have to worry about
	the games people play...

Chorus 2x Got to be careful today
Got to find a better way...

Sun will rise on a brighter day
Teach the youth how to kneel and pray
Peace and harmony will rain their way
This is the love we need today.

Got to be careful today
Got to find a better way...

Written by Edward Eddy © 11/10/06

Don't Want To Be

Chorus 2x   I don't want to be
                  A victim in the system

Vs 1   They're trying to keep us down
                  But we're not going to fret or frown
                  We can gain the knowledge
                  To wear the Crown.

Vs 2   Wisdom is the key, the key to life
                  And it's a must, that we need the
                  knowledge to end the strife
                  We walk by faith and not by sight
                  That's why we need, to
                  keep up the good fight

Chorus 2x   I don't want to be
                  A victim in the system

Bridge	*That is why, I'm so optimistic*
	Because I have to be realistic
	I don't want to be another statistic
	That's why I have to be mystic.
Vs 3	*The devil pushes his people*
	to keep us bound
	And you will know if you
	just look around
	The Bible shows us how love abounds
	*If it's love of **God**, where*
	the peace is found
Chorus 2x	*I don't want to be*
	A victim in the system

Written by Edward Eddy © 07/14/06

Shining Star

When times are hard
And life seems rough
And dark clouds are on the way

Just think of me
And I'll be there
To brighten up your day

A brother's love
Can know no bounds
With a wonderful sister like you

You're a shining star
My evening light
In everything I do.

By: Edward Eddy

It's All About You

Hook	It's all about you
Chorus	And the things you do
Verse 1:	I like the way
	You wear your hair
	It shows me lady
	That you care
Chorus:	It's all about you
	And the things you do
Verse 2:	I like the way
	You smile at me
	Make me feel
	So wild and free
Chorus:	It's all about you
	And the things you do

Verse 3:   I like the smell
                Of your perfume
                Like sweet jasmine
                In full bloom

Chorus: It's all about you
                And the things you do

Verse 4:   One more thing
                You should know
                I'm gonna get you
                Before I go

                Written By: Edward Eddy ©11/09/05

You're Mine

My passion for you runs so deep,
MY love for you I want to keep.
Every day, Baby, of each long, lonely week,
My love for your grows only more sweet

I remember so well the day we met,
Your sweet, lovely smile I can never forget.
Time stopped as I gazed into your eyes,
Lost in your loveliness, and not knowing why.

Both thinking the same, hearts beating in time,
Breaths we take together let's
our chemistry entwine.
Holding your body, sets my soul on fire,
But touching your mind is really my desire

Though we're not together, we're really never apart,
Our love burns forever deep within my heart.
One spirit, one soul, one body, by design,
The Lord decreed this; I'm yours, you're mine.

Written By: Edward Eddy ©10/18/05

I Want To Chill

Chorus 3x: I just want to chill
                       With you

Verse1:   Me and you tonight
                       We can make things right
                       Baby we can untwine
                       And have a real good time...

Chorus 3x: I just want to chill

Verse 2:   We don't need to know stress
                       Let's forget about the rest
                       I just want the best
                       Cause Lady we'll be blessed...

Bridge 1x: I think of you every night
                       And I want you in my arms
                       Honey as my wife...

Chorus 3x: I just want to chill

Verse 3:	I want to make you mine
	Cause your love is divine – genuine
	We could wine and dine
	Till the end of time
Chorus 3x:	I just want to chill
Verse 4:	Till the morning sunrise
	My love will be a surprise
	Baby when I look into your eyes
	I begin to fantasize
	That the world is yours and mine...

Written By: Edward Eddy © 05/06/05

People Of The World

Chorus 2:   People of the world
       People of the world

Verse 1   No need for bombing
       No need for hijacking
       People are dying
       People are crying
       For what we are lacking
       Cause we are...

Chorus 2x: People of the world
       People of the world

Verse 2:   What we need is more heroism
       We need no more terrorism
       What we need is location
       Between **God** and each nation
       That will be such a great revelation...

Bridge1x: If we join hands in unity
       There will be peace and harmony
       We can be friends and have close ties
       There is no reason that we have to die
       The world will be a better place
       For you and me...

Chorus 2x:	*People of the world*
	People of the world
Verse 3:	*There's plenty to share*
	If we all stop and care
	No need for poverty
	Reach out to your brother
	Let's all help one another
	There's beauty for all to see
	That's beauty for our reality
	Cause we are...
Chorus 2x:	*People of the world*
	People of the world

Written By: Edward Eddy © 07/064/05

My Dedication To
Mr. Hamilton's Institution

Mr. Hamilton is both teacher and friend
If you open up your heart and mind
He will be there till the end.

He teaches academics, and also life skills
His students take life more seriously
They don't have time to sit and chill.

In working to get a better education
They grow in leaps and bounds
Learning helps then better their situation.

We all need to seek a higher elevation
And at the Hamilton Institute
You will get some inspiration.

At the Institute, there's no
room for discrimination
For his heart is filled with fellowship
For every color and creed in the nation.

He help students gain a solid
education position
To help their children and the family
Not being stopped by opposition.

Mr. Hamilton teaches us to
make sound decision
Achieving higher goals, to
the mountain top
To become better educated
takes work and precision

Mr. Hamilton can help us to
improve our education
He's the foundation, backbone
and cornerstone
His knowledge sets the example
for our generation.

Written By: Edward Eddy © 01/02/05

A Dedication to
Mr. Lorenzo Hamilton

Manners Mr. Hamilton will never neglect
He is always ready to show you respect,
He is a teacher and a really good friend
He will help and stand by you until the end.

Not just a friend he's a father figure
Inspiring young and old to want to deliver,
The love and compassion that he shares
Shows us just how much he really cares.

He doesn't do it all, he's good at delegating
Keeping involved and fully relating.
He motivates his students to participate
In classes and activities that are really great.

Mr. Hamilton you're a man of true integrity
You stand for learning, justice and liberty,
You're a true role-model in the community
Living by the values of love, faith and unity.

Your wife and son can be proud of you
Appreciating all the good things that you do,
In all you strive for you have a good report
Your family stands by you to show support.

Written By: Edward Eddy © 01/02/07

Each One Teach One

By Edward Eddy © 02/04/99

Chorus 2x   *Each one reach one,*
                       each one teach one.

Vs 1   *Raise up your youth in a Godly way*
                       Teach them how to kneel an pray
                       Show them that the Father
                       is here everyday
                       Don't ever let them go astray

Chorus 2x   *Each one reach one,*
                       each one teach one.

Vs. 2   *Raise up your youth in*
                       an educated way
                       Show them that crime on
                       the streets don't pay
                       Always take time to
                       hear what they say
                       Don't ever let then go astray

Chorus 2x	*Each one reach one,*
	each one teach one.
Vs. 3	*We must be strong to do the work*
	Of the Father up above
	Show them the path they must take
	To avoid making big mistakes
Chorus 2x	*Each one reach one,*
	each one teach one.
Vs 4	*Raise up your youth and*
	make them cautious
	That they are dying from
	lack of knowledge
	We know weapon that
	creates the condition
	Keep them away from
	the "tell-a-lie-vision"

Chorus 2x   *Each one reach one,*
each one teach one.

Vs. 5   *Keep them away from the*
crack and cocaine
Those are the things that
will ruin their brain
So they know what's wrong
and know what's right
So they won't need to fuss and fight.

Oh Heavenly Father

Chorus 2x:

Oh heavenly Father
I am with Thee
And I want to Thank You
For savimg me...

Verse 1:

When I come to you Lord
Down on my knees
You picked me up Lord
And gave me peace...

Chorus 2x:

Oh heavenly Father
I am with Thee
And I want to Thank You
For savimg me...

Verse 2:

For all my pain Lord
And suffering
You gave me joy Lord
To stand again...

By Edward Eddy © 01/04/1996

A Gift From God

Women are a gift from **God**, very special treasures
Godmade woman to make man whole,
To complete him, and fill his soul

Men are the ones made to plant the seed
He made woman to bring forth the fruits,
Together we're the next generations' root

Give women respect as our Queens
They're more precious than diamond and pearls,
Worth more than anything in the world

She's a precious and desirable Queen
It's her that can make men Kings,
Let's get rid of those negative things.

They need to be treated as if they're Queens
Beautiful, proud, courageous, and gifted,
It's by them a man's heart is lifted.

They deserve the utmost respect
Remember gentlemen, women are treasures,
They bring us such beauty and pleasure.

By Edward Eddy © 10/04/06

God's Treasure

Trust God for your queen
And by all means he will give you
The desire of your dreams.

Trust Godfor your queen
And you will see he is faithful and just
To give you what you need.

She is a Lady of beauty and compassion
Long black silky hair eyes glittering like the stars
With a spirit so holy.

God's own creation
Demonstrated for man to see in a living being
Trust Godfor your queen.

A woman of wisdom
Knowledge and understanding
Who stands by her man day by day?
Knowing Jesus is the one who paved our way.

Trust Godfor your dream
Trust Godfor your queen.

By: Edward Eddy 06/07/07

"Women Are Treasure"

Women are treasure, they bring so much pleasure
I think of all women as gifts from **God**.
The Lord has blessed us with
women to make us whole,
And we should love them from depths of our soul.

We are the one that plant the seed,
They are the one the one that brings the fruit;
The generation of each root.

Women are more precious than
rubies, diamonds and pearls
And can be compared to nothing in this world.
Let us give them the utmost respect
That our queens deserve.

She is a precious feminine queen
That is here to stand for her almighty king
Let's get rid of all those negative things.

Courageous, proud, beautiful and gifted
Every day they deserve the utmost
of our precious time.

Don't forget gentleman, women are treasures
That brings so much beauty and pleasure.

By: Edward Eddy

God Will Be There For You

Chorus 2x

God will be there for you (2x\)
When you are falling
That I know...

Verse 1:

When the world seems
hard to bear
Count on **God** and He'll be there
And all we got to do
And all we got to do
I put our trust in the Lord...

Verse 2:

Jesus died on the cross
To cover every one of us
Let's give Him the
Glory and praise
His Holy Name we magnify...

Chorus 2x

God will be there for you (2x\)
When you are falling
That I know...

By Edward Eddy © 02/01/1996

Beyond Compare

Never forgetting to care for me
Always there to comfort me
Only you can truly know me
Mother you, you're beyond compare
I truly love you.

Each one greet one
Do good have fun
Don't be bad one
You'll be blessed one.

By Edward Eddy © 06/10/107

Birds

Birds can fly
Birds can sing
But birds can't
Remember anything!
But I can!

By Edward Eddy © 09/11/06

Spirit So Sweet

A gracious woman with
A spirit so sweet
No finer a lady could you
Ever hope to meet
She taught me to use my
Knowledge and will
I will love her forever until.

By Edward Eddy 05/07/06

Truly Desire

By the sparkle
In your eyes
I am mesmerized
I can see
The zest and the beauty
You possess inside
You startle me
And cause my sense to rise
Oh what a pleasant surprise
I was tantalized by
The shape of your body
I truly desire
Mind, soul, and body.

By Edward Eddy © 09/10/06

Gentle Flower

You are like a gentle Flower
You are lovelier by the hour
You are into my life and light my fire
You are everything my heart desires

Not only lovely you're gentle and kind
Thoughts of you rest easy on my mind
The meekest, sweetest lady I'll ever find
Your precious spirit keeps my heart entwined.

By: Edward Eddy 12/21/2008

Special Father

Very special in my life
Exceptional at all you do
Ready to help all you can
Naturally steady and true
Only you in Caribbean water
No other is like you, my Father.

By Edward Eddy © 09/09/06

True Light

Because you taught me
Only things that were right
Seeing the good in me
Showing me the true light.

I love you Boss.

By Edward Eddy © 09/08/06

"Dark Light"

The candle that I lit sheds no light at all;
Doesn't even cast a shadow on this empty wall;
I ask the question where I went wrong.
Tears are my only answer all the lonely night long.

For each candle lit, another hard lesson learned,
All night I lay sleepless, I only tossed and turned.
Freedom I'll never know, never have a chance to see,
My candle burns so low; the future is dark for me

I have so much to gain; I am able now to know,
It's only through hope and grace I can grow,
My eyes have seen the light, His blood upon the sod,
I am humbled by the sight and I give myself to **God**.

He will keep my candle burning
through the lonely night
My heart is yearning, to this time do it right.
I live in peace today for he guides me every night
He shows me the true way to be
welcome in his sight.

By: Edward Eddy 1/2/1997

"Freedom"

Freedom is only a hands reach away
Just as it will be on Judgment Day,

Freedom is always a beautiful sight
But some feel it wouldn't be right,

Freedom is something we all seem to seek
No matter if it's behind bars or in our sleep.

Freedom too many of us is just a seven letter word
Because guilty, guilty, guilty is all we heard.

Freedom for some of us will eventually come true
But it doesn't really matter until
that someone is you.

Freedom has a language all on its own
It comes in laughter, tears and a cry to be home

Freedom is a blessing that comer
from the creator above
Because no matter what our wrong
is His blessing of love.

With freedom being only a hands reach away
Some of us will never reach it until judgment day.

By Edward Eddy

Dear Mother

A woman who is courageous
and gifted
A special lady who God
has lifted.
You know that in the world
there is no other
Who is as precious and sweet
as my Dear Mother

By Edward Eddy © 09/06/06

Family Love

How special the love of this family has been
You have stayed with me through thick and thin,
Distance means nothing for you live in my heart
Though we're not together, we are never apart.

You're Uncles and Aunts on my family tree
But sometimes you're more like parents to me,
Mom and Dad have a special part to play
But you have helped me every step of the way.

By: Edward Eddy 11/16/2008

Rare and Unique

You're so beautiful, rare and unique;
You're the special woman I truly seek
All of your mind, body and soul
Are what I need to make me whole

Softly and lovely as two honey dew that rest
The perfect shaped and sized breasts.
The whiteness of your teeth, a row of pearls
Your soft silky hair, and the way it curls.

Your womanly fragrance, rare and exciting
Your lovely lips are so kissable and inviting.
The way you stand, the sway of your walk
As I watched your movement, I can hardly talk.

Even though you are miles away
You capture my heart and brighten up each day
And if that isn't enough you see
I'll show you more of what you mean to me.

The curling hair around your sweet valley
Flowing with juice like milk and honey
Opening the softness of rose petaled lips
Sweet ecstasy comes to my fingertips.

By Edward Eddy © 05/07/07

Light and Goodness

Sweetly singing as morning comes
Everyone listens, a new day begun
Youth and beauty flow in your song
Body and soul, we all sing along
In times of trouble, you leave n doubt
Light and goodness will always win out.

Rising to heaven your whispered prayer
Heaven awaits to ease your care
Yours are the hands that hold the truth
Mine are the ears of undisciplined youth
Educate me in the way I must go
Really and truly, I must say it's so.

By Edward Eddy © 05/04/07

The Truth

In this dark and dreary world
Bearing in mind that Jesus lives within
Our lives we always seem to be in a swirl,
The reason is that we live in sin.

If we just call on the Lord
He gives us joy and peace abound.
We have his promise in his word
If we only turn our lives around.

Give up your times of toil and pain
Turn to the one whose love is true.
Walk in the way of God again
And turn your gray skies to blue.

Though the world seems so cold
And clouds cover the sun
With faith in **God** we can be bold
Knowing beauty has only begun.

God's love is our sunshine
Dark skies turn away
With life in the true vine
Jesus love will always stay.

By: Edward Eddy 6/7/05

"Dear Lord"

Dear Lord: *You say ask and you shall receive,*
Lord hear my prayers as I bow to my knees.
Dear Lord: *I come to you in tears of prayers*
It's my mom who needs your care.
Dear Lord: *My prayers remain the same*
Would you please remove all her hurt and pain.
Dear Lord: *Please hear my prayer*
And place her in your care.
Dear Lord: *Show her that your*
presence is always near
No matter if you're on earth or in the air.
Dear Lord: *Show her that this is not the end*
As long as she holds you deep within.
Dear Lord: *bless her soul with all your love*
And all the loving things from Above.
Dear Lord: *I know you can hear my cry*
She's not ready to say goodbye.
Dear Lord: *Please do whatever you can*
Because my mom needs your loving hand.

By: Edward Eddy 11/02/95

For Everyone To See
Shining Light

As the years flow slowly by,
And clouds obscure the sun,
At times I feel too sad to cry,
All hopes fading one by one.

My thoughts have just to turn to you
The One Who gave me life,
The one who's heart is always true
In good times and in strife.

Then clouds give way to shining light
Sadness turns to glee,
My love for you is always bright
For everyone to see.

By Edward Eddy 09/05/06

Man with a Mind

A man with a mind
Just sitting and wasting his time
Why can't we all dig deep inside
And realize that we all hold a surprise.

God created us all in his own image
And a touch of his son deep inside
So why can't we all realize
That we have the power deep inside.

A man with a mind
Who trust **God** and uses his time
Will find the treasure hidden inside
Even though lies cover his eyes.

Though we be men in disguise
A man with a mind sees in life the Devine
Trusts **God** and doesn't waste time
Knows He created us all with brilliance in mind.

A man of wisdom and knowledge
A man with a mind.

By: Edward Eddy

Juicy Fruits

Even though you are so far away
Each moment of you brightens my day
You captured my heart and that is why
Sweet memories of you make me sigh.

Your voluptuous body, you silken hair
Like tropical fruits and blossom rare
Your up turned breasts are a lovely sight
Two perfect melons just for my delight.

Your womanly flower, sweet center of bliss
Like an orchid opening to the sun's kiss
Hides sweet nectar deeply within
To be loved and savored again and again.

By Edward Eddy © 05/04/07

Pleasant Person

Pleasant person you seem to be
Always striving to show respect
Trying to love all humanity
Righteously doing what is correct
Intentionally giving of your self
Caring, and sharing, and kind
Kid Brother I like your mind.

Each one greet one
Do good have fun
Don't be bad one
You be blessed one.

By Edward Eddy © 05/04/07

Special Person

Special person you are
Everyone loves your smile
Liking to drive in your car
Walking isn't your style
Young women like you by far
Now that's why you are so wild.

Each one greet one
Do good have fun
Don't be bad one
You be blessed one.

By Edward Eddy © 05/04/07

You Are Precious

Equally dear you are my son
Very precious the youngest one
Always you'll have this special place
Now I'll be happy when I see your face.

Each one great one
Do good have fun
Don't be bad one
You'll be blessed one.

By: Edward Eddy 06/10/07

Very Unique

Very unique, inquiring mind
Intelligence second to name
Naturally loving, cheerful and kind
Caring deeply for everyone
Educated, dedicated, on your own way
Nothing can stop you for long
Tough minded and spiritually strong.

Each one greet one
Do good have fun
Don't be bad one
You be blessed one.

By Edward Eddy © 05/04/07

I Wonder

Vs. 1

I wonder when will
I see you again
I wonder what it will be
like when we meet again
I can picture you smiling
face in the back of my mind
As I think about the love
we shared back in time.

(Chorus 2x)

I think about you every
day in so many ways
And what I feel is
deep in my soul
I know that it's real that's
why I've got to tell you
That your love makes
me whole.

Vs.2

I wonder if our love
will be the same
I wonder what It'll be like
when I call your name
I still remember that
day you went away
And the look that you
had on your face
And I don't mind about
the way I feel inside
Because no one can
take your place...

Written by Edward Eddy © 01/07/1996

Time and Distance

(Chorus 2x) Time and distance do not matter
       Love is always and forever.

Vs. 1   When I wake up in the morning
       And I see your lovely face
       Love for you I freshly forming
       Love the time cannot erase.

(Chorus 2x) Time and distance do not matter
       Love is always and forever.

Vs. 2   Every time that I am with you
       We always have a lot of fun
       Showing me that your love is true
       Warms my heart just like the sun.

(Chorus 2x) Time and distance do not matter
       Love is always and forever.

Written by Edward Eddy © 07/10/07

I Think of You

Every day I think of you
Don't know when I'll see you
Within me you're a special part
Always here deep in my heart
Rain or shine, stormy or clear
Daily I want to have you near.

Each one greet one
Do good have fun
Don't be bad one
You'll be blessed one.

Just as father carries this name
Rightfully, first son has the same.

Written by Edward Eddy © 0/10/07

African Queen

Chorus 2X   *Shine on Shine on my*
African Queen
For the light of your love
sparkles on me,

Verse 1   *My days and my nights*
are shining so bright
Because of your love makes
everything all right
Each morning that I rise I
look in your eyes your
Big precious smile makes
everything alright.

Chorus 2X   *Shine on Shine my*
African on Queen
For the light of your love
sparkles on me,

Verse 2	Baby you're more precious than diamonds and pearls That's why you are my favorite girl. Honey you more costly than silver or gold And I love your sugar with all my heart and soul.
Chorus 2X	Shine on Shine my African on Queen For the light of your love sparkles on me,
Verse 3	You're the woman of my dreams So lean and supreme that's why You are my African Queen.
Chorus 2X	Shine on Shine my African on Queen For the light of your love sparkles on me,

Bridge   *Girl I love your tender touch*
and it isn't about lust
Come into my arms its
love you can trust,
I am down on my knees and
I am begging you please
Girl stay with me until eternity.

Chorus 2X   *Shine on Shine my*
African on Queen
For the light of your love
sparkles on me,

By: Edward Eddy"95"

I Remember You

Each time I remember you
Love and joy some shining through
Often I see you in my mind's eye
Never changing though time goes by

Each one greet one
Do good have fun
Don't be bad one
You'll be blessed one.

By Edward Eddy © 06/10/07

In The Garden

In the garden of my heart
You're the sweetest of blooms
In the mansion of my soul
You're the chiefest of rooms
In the field of my existence
You're the choicest of grains
In the heavens of my future
You're the precious, loving rains.

By Edward Eddy © 06/10/07

Long to Hold

With all the women in the world
I'm truly blessed that you're my girl
I love you dear for who you are.
Whenever you're at, near or far.
I love all of you, mind, body, and soul.
All of you, is what I long to hold.

By Edward Eddy © 06/10/07

Only One of You

I would never find
Another lady like you

I would like spending
With a woman like you.

Cause I know God
Only made one of you.

By Edward Eddy © 06/21/07

The Honey Bee

In the flowers of your garden
I want to be the honey bee
Sipping the sweet nectar
Of your flowering love for me.

By Edward Eddy © 06/10/07

Love and Happiness

Every day I think of love and happiness
Don't think about the pain or sadness
Want to get away from all the madness
And I want to indulge in all gladness
Return to my favorite youthful years
Don't want to shed anymore tears.

Each one greet one
Do good have fun
Don't be bad one
You'll be blessed one.

Surely father of the family tree
Reaching out to secure posterity

By Edward Eddy © 06/10/07

Consequences and Choices

In this world of consequences and choices
We must listen to the small voices.
Deep inside thoughts of God son still resides
But, the enemy also lurks and hides
Feeding us deceptions and lies.

In God eyes we are the sole prize
Please listen and drop your pride
The choices you make pave the way
To be a better future when you kneel and pray
To walk with God and not go astray.

If I choose to do wrong
My life on earth will not be long.
The consequences are a fact of life
The eyes of an enemy can cut like a knife.
Choose peace with God, or trouble and strife.

The peace of God overcomes all things
Brings songs of joy to your heart strings
So, remember my friend each and every day
You're never as tall as when you kneel and pray.
I hope you listen to the words I just say.

By Edward Eddy "96"